SING OUT LOUD

BOOK IV

Owning the Stage

Jaime Vendera & Anne Loader McGee

VP

Vendera
Publishing

Vendera Publishing

Interior Design by Daniel Middleton | www.scribefreelance.com
Cover Design by Molly Burnside | www.crosssidedesigns.com
Photo detail: Abby Hunter, Emi Jo Hammond, Jaime Vendera,
Kirk Gilbert, and Tommie Armstrong
Copyright © 2011 by Kevin Hoops | Impressive Studios
Cartoon Illustrations by Jerry Bingham | www.JerryBingham.com
Audio examples recorded by Jaime Vendera

ISBN: 978-1-936307-11-1

Published in the United States of America

Books by Jaime Vendera
*Raise Your Voice Second Edition
*The Ultimate Breathing Workout
*The Ultimate Vocal Workout Diary
*Voice RX
*Vocal RESET
*Extreme Scream series
*Online Teaching Secret Revealed
*Unleash Your Creative Mindset

Books by Anne McGee
*Strengthening Your Singing Voice (Elizabeth Sabine)
*The Mystery at Marlatt Manor
*Anni's Attic

Contents

Introduction

Welcome back to the fourth installment of the *Sing Out Loud* series. Bet you can't believe how much your voice has improved! What a difference it makes once you've discovered the secrets of correct vocal technique, developed vibrato, added emotion, taken the time to discover your own sound, and begun a daily singing and practice regimen. But there's no sense in putting all this effort into developing a great voice if you forget about developing a great stage presence to go with it. If you're going to perform, you definitely want to be your shining best, so now we're going to show you how.

You're about to be introduced to the *Sing Out Loud* performance system; a 'crash-course' designed to get you on stage and owning the audience in record time. We'll do this through a series of eleven intense assignments for mastering the stage as well as mastering the microphone, and conquering stage fright. This is the shortest book in the series, consisting of only four chapters, but each one gets right to the point. No play time, all work. If you want to be a great performer and own the stage, you must follow the lesson plan in this book. So get ready for non-stop assignments that will give you the guidance to discover the true performer in you.

Chapter 1
Owning the Stage

The best way to develop your stage presence is to dive right into it with an assignment.

Assignment #1—Studying Stage Moves

For your first assignment, you'll need to head over to *YouTube* and search for ten live performance videos of some of your favorite artists. Make sure you view a variety of artists, not just ten videos from one band. Next open up a blank document on your computer and write down all the cool moves you notice the artists do in their videos. Note what moves you liked and what moves you'd like to be able to do.

Artists will perform a variety of moves on stage, many with professionally choreographed dances to more simplistic things like closing their eyes at certain key phrases, pointing to the audience, holding the microphone out so the audience can sing along, even doing physical back flips—the list goes on and on. By the end of this assignment, you should have a pretty extensive list of cool stage moves you'll want to try out.

Assignment #2—Testing Out Those Stage Moves

Now try each move on the list you've just created. It's important to see what you look like so use the mirror to do this. What moves seem easy? What moves look cool? It's important to be able to pick apart each move and learn the ones that will work for you on stage. Don't expect to have a move down right away as this is simply the point where you get an idea of whether any of them are right for you or not. And it's not considered stealing—there are no new moves, and everyone learns how to perform from watching others.

We put emphasis on using a mirror because it's your personal guide to vocal and performance success. From now on you'll use the mirror for two separate purposes. One, as your personal vocal coach to make sure you don't make any physical mistakes such as looking up or opening your mouth while you're doing exercises, and two, as a guide to teach you how to move on stage.

From this point on begin practicing in a mirror every single time you sing. That way you'll not only catch any bad vocal habits, but you'll develop tons of cool stage moves. If you catch yourself making a goofy face while singing, make a mental note to avoid that face in the future. Maybe you notice you lean way back for all the high notes. The mirror will help you figure out how far back to lean, how far apart to spread your legs, etc. Hopefully you have a full body mirror so you can see yourself from every angle. If you have the chance to use a mirrored studio, that would be even better.

The *Sing Out Loud* performance system believes it's just as important to train your entire body for a performance as it is to train your voice. Plus, your physical movements during a performance can affect your voice, so it's important to learn what works for you right from the start. Remember that if your posture is out of whack, then some part of your anatomy is not taking part in the desire to sing.

As stated earlier in the *Sing Out Loud* system, imagine a string attached to the crown of your head that's pulling you up. We don't want you to stand stiffly throughout your whole performance, but if you remember the head-pulling string idea it will help immensely with poor posture. So roll around on the stage, do cart wheels, slide on your knees if you want, but go back to correct posture every now and then.

Assignment #3—Checking Out Your Own Moves

Now it's time to perform. Turn on your *Sing Out Loud* practice song and stand in front of a mirror. It's time to rock out. Go nuts as you sing your song. Use some of the dance moves you've been practicing and add new ones. It may take several songs before you find your flow, but that's to be expected. The goal of this assignment is to figure out the cool/non-cool moves as you sing.

Once you decide what you'd like to do, turn on your computer and start another document. Write down your cool moves, even adding the best ones from *Assignment #1*. Maybe you dropped to your knees and wailed and you thought it looked cool. Add that to the cool list. If you noticed you repeatedly made a goofy face that made you look like some cartoon character, put it on the list of moves you want to avoid. You can also videotape yourself to check out your moves from different angles. Combine the mirror and videotaping to truly discover what you look like.

In order to become a superstar performer, you must own the stage from the moment you step onto it until the moment you leave it. So from now on, every time you perform, whether in your church choir, school play, karaoke, or in front of your own band, consider yourself a "SUPERSTAR" and walk onto the center stage the way a true superstar would.

Speaking of a school play, performing live is very much like acting. You're playing a role with every song you sing. Learn your role and become so good at the character the audience will believe that's who you are.

Assignment #4—Acting it Out

Now let's take those cool moves from the last assignment and put them to use. Listen to your *Sing Out Loud* practice song paying close attention to the lyrics. Think of all your moves, and be ready to add some new ones to help explain the story in the song. Imagine you're a character in an upcoming play. What moves would you use to explain this character to your audience as you sing? That's the goal for this assignment. Watch yourself in the mirror, video tape your performance and study your new moves.

Assignment #5—Performance Mapping

Now that you have some acting experience under your belt, let's make sure you remember the moves for your 'role' in the song. Remember your song map from *Sing Out Loud Book III*? Well, you can also create *performance* maps that allow you to choreograph your moves throughout the entire song. This is what most pop artists do. They have a choreographer who creates dance movements based on the interpretation of the lyrics.

Remember you're playing a role. How do you learn a role? By studying the script and understanding the nuances of a character, or in our case, reviewing the song by doing the following:

- Write out the lyrics
- Figure out what story the lyrics are trying to tell
- Analyze what emotions are present in the song. What's the mood?
- What character is singing the song? (Hero, villain, boyfriend, girlfriend, etc.)
- What movements on stage would best express the character? Would crawling on your hands and knees express sadness or urgency, or doing a back flip during the guitar solo show how excited the character has become?
- What individual words can you use to create a stage move? For example, if the word "sleeping" was in a line, could you tilt your head and close your eyes as you sing that word? Verbs and nouns can easily be turned into new stage moves, whether it's a word like 'sleeping', 'heart', 'crying', etc. When performing, your entire body should become a tool that's telling the story.

Looks like it's time to create your first performance map. Don't worry; a performance map is much easier to create than a song map. Simply highlight the word you want to turn into a stage move. For instance, in the words 'hearts' and 'beating' from the song "Hey Lady" by *Thriving Ivory*, you could place your hand on your chest and tap to express that your heart is still beating. If you want to add a move that has nothing to do with the meaning of a word, such as running from the left side of the stage to the right side, then standing in place on every chorus, just add a side note on your map to remind you of that decision. If you combine your performance map with your song map, always highlight your performance words and side notes so you don't get confused between the lyrics and the moves. Here's an example:

F#   F#   F   F   D#-D#   D#   D# D# D#↗g#   F
She checks her pulse~~~ 'got-ta know~~ if her heart's still (hand at heart)

D#-C#
beating~~' (walk slowly across the stage)

Here we added to our song map from *Sing Out Loud Book III*. As you can see, the highlighted words after the word "beating" refers to a move you can make. You can create endless moves, but it will take practice to figure out which ones work best. Moving around as you sing will soon feel like second nature and allow you to get into performance mode way before you hit the stage.

Bottom line here is, every song should tell a story. Every movement you make, every expression on your face, and every tone you vocally release must express your character.

Now you're developing and adding to two bags of tricks—your vocal bag and your performance bag.

Assignment #6—Finding Your Flow

But adding more things to your vocal performance bag of tricks isn't enough. You must develop the ability to perform these moves smoothly and in perfect timing. To keep your timing locked in place you must find the flow and feel of the rhythm of the music. And you must know the correct tempo of the song. You can easily find and keep the rhythm by feeling the beat of the kick drum vibrating in your body, and by listening to the bass guitar. The job of the drums and bass are to keep the timing, so if you follow these two instruments you'll never go wrong. Tap your foot to the beat of the music if this helps keep you in rhythm. Take control and count it down with your band. If you have a good band, they'll get in sync with your tempo immediately.

For this assignment go back and listen to your practice song and begin tapping your foot to the rhythm. Continue doing this through the entire song. If you lose the rhythm, find it again, and continue. Go through the song as many times as needed until you can keep the rhythm going from start to finish. If it tires your foot, tap on your thigh with your hand instead.

Assignment #7—Practicing with a Metronome

If you still have difficulty keeping time, you may want to consider purchasing a device called a 'metronome'. You can either find one at a music store or buy an app on iTunes. Go to the Internet and type in, "Online Metronome". You'll find several free choices to download.

Whether you get an actual metronome or download an app, play around with the speed until you find a beginning speed that is easy to tap your foot to without getting off rhythm. Once you feel at ease doing this, then try tapping every other beat.

Now that you've found your rhythm, it's important to note singing is a very energetic activity so learn to make small body movements throughout your song so you can maintain that energy. If the song is an outrageous, full-of-energy anthem, then you may feel the need to do some head banging. The important thing is to reserve your energy because moving around on stage can soon wear you out. If you start to get out of breath and it affects your singing, you need to slow down. Stand still while singing for a few minutes or change your moves back to small ones. You can add more energetic moves once you've recovered.

Your goal is to maintain your voice throughout the entire show no matter what your actions. The last thing you want to do is end up lip-syncing a performance because you can't keep up the energy. Knowing *how* to move around the stage with small body movements and *when* to head bang is extremely important in maintaining your voice.

Assignment #8—Cardio Singing

If you become short-winded as you practice your stage moves, boy, do we have the cure for you. It's called cardio singing and it's performed on a treadmill. Fill your mp3 player with the songs you regularly sing, grab some headphones and get ready to sing while you run a minimum of thirty minutes. You can start with ten minutes, and then increase it in five-minute increments until it becomes easier. Singing while on the treadmill will not only help your fatigue problem, it will also make you a stronger singer by building your diaphragm and abdominal muscles. Make sure to breathe correctly as you run. If you need to take a singing break then do so, but keep running and jump back in when you can. In a few weeks, you'll have lungs of steel.

Assignment #9—It's all in the Eyes

Awesome, now you have some great moves and also powerful lungs to back those moves up. Still the secret to owning the stage lies in a singer's eyes. By connecting through eye contact with your listeners you will captivate them and make fans for life. In this assignment we'll go back to the mirror. Stare intensely into your own eyes as if you were staring at someone else. Then sing and imagine this person is your #1 fan. Do your stage moves, pay attention to your vocal technique, and keep that direct eye contact. Add other moves such as pointing to yourself in the mirror, or holding out an imaginary microphone, as if enticing the person in the reflection to sing along with you. This assignment will teach you a lot about how to interact with an audience.

You should spend several weeks working through these assignments to master your stagecraft. They are the heart of the *Sing Out Loud* performance system and if you work hard enough, you'll hit the stage filled with lots of confidence and tricks up your sleeve. Speaking of the stage, now it's time for the last assignment in this chapter.

Assignment #10—Taking it to the Stage

Standing in front of a mirror will only get you so far. The best way to become a real live performer is to perform live. Look for every opportunity to do this because you need to practice your moves in front of a live audience.

Keep your eyes moving as you perform; look at your audience row by row and then from side to side. Don't make actual eye contact, but look at the forehead area. If you do make eye contact, that's fine but quickly move on. Staring at the forehead will stop you from getting distracted by wondering what they're thinking about. It will also allow you to move easily from person to person. Make your voice carry through each individual all the way to the last row. By aiming your voice to the back of the room, your sound will come out of you effortlessly and be felt by everyone present. Give the audience the feeling you're friends with every one of them by connecting with your eyes.

Learn to be comfortable on stage. Your mouth should feel moist with saliva when you sing. If you have a dry mouth and throat, this is a sign you're nervous or in doubt about your ability to keep everyone's attention. Every performer gets nervous. It's a natural thing and not a problem, but if your mouth and throat continue to stay dry well into your song, then you're letting nervousness take over.

Keep this in mind. The brain will release the same chemicals into your body whether you're nervous or excited. If you can think about feeling excited as opposed to feeling fearful then you can use that same energy to your advantage. We explain nervousness and stage fright in Chapter 3, *Conquering Performance Jitters,* and ways to keep the voice moist in Chapter 4, *Taking Care of Your Instrument.*

We highly suggest you practice often to develop a natural feel for performance. This includes practicing by yourself as well as with your band (if you have a band). You also want to begin practicing your song with a microphone, regardless of whether or not it is plugged in. Microphone technique is an art form in itself. And speaking of that, let's spend the next chapter discussing correct microphone technique.

Chapter 2
Mastering Microphone Technique

To become an awesome performer, you must not only be able to sing and move well, but also understand about microphone technique. A singer's voice is considered an instrument so the microphone is an extension of that instrument. Knowing how to use a microphone correctly is crucial to a good performance. Note the following seven points:

1. Finding the right microphone

As a singer there are several reasons why it's important to have your own microphone. Depending on your voice, one type of microphone can make you sound quite different from another. You should go to a music store and try out different microphones. Find one that sounds good when you speak or sing through it. Keep in mind there are other factors that can make you sound good, such as the EQ settings on the store's soundboard, or a vocal effects processor with reverb and other effects. When you try out a microphone in a store, though, make sure to tell the salesperson you'd like to hear the microphone dry, that means with no EQ or sound effects.

There are a host of microphones on the market that can cost anywhere from fifty dollars up to thousands. Some of the more popular brands include: Blue, TC Helicon, Shure, EV, Audio Technica, and Sampson. It's not necessary to spend hundreds of dollars, but don't cheat yourself either by buying a really cheap one. Most decent microphones run at least a hundred bucks. Some more expensive stage microphones require what is called *phantom power* in order to work, but the type and price of a microphone does not always equate to a sound you will like. We know many big artists who prefer cheaper microphones for both stage and recording. If price is a concern, look online at auction sites such as "eBay" to find a reasonably priced microphone.

Another reason to have your own microphone is for sanitary purposes. Who wants to use a microphone that contains spit and germs from someone else's mouth? Keep it clean by occasionally wiping the top of the mic with a rag dipped in rubbing alcohol. You can also buy a cheap foam windscreen cover that slips over the top of your microphone to help protect it from your own saliva and spit.

2. Holding the microphone

Now that you have a microphone, you need to learn how to hold it. Sounds simple, right? Not always. Learning to tame the hand that holds your microphone can be a chore. Don't wave the microphone around or move it away from your face when you sing. It will make your sound fade in and out and also distract the audience from your performance by having to focus on its every move. Keep it within a few inches of your mouth, not off to one side. Some singers prefer to work with the mic on a stand, which is fine. Others allow their audience to sing along on certain lines by extending the mic towards the crowd. This is fine too, but generally when you sing, you need to keep it close to your mouth.

3. Eating the microphone

The way you sing into your microphone affects the way sound comes out through the speakers. Lots of rock singers almost devour their mic in order to get a more distorted sound. This is fine for songs that need distortion or an "in-your-face" type sound, but because sound automatically travels down, it's best to adjust

the microphone to a 45-degree angle to the mouth and maintain a steady two to three inch distance from it.

4. Wired or wireless microphone

Using a wired or wireless microphone is up to you. Some people even prefer a headset with one. If you plan to move around the stage a lot or add choreographed dance moves, a wireless microphone might be the best choice, but they do cost more. In most instances, a regular wired microphone is sufficient. If needed, add a twenty-foot microphone cable to allow you to move around. There are many companies that produce awesome wireless microphones and headsets. If you already own a wired microphone, then you might want to consider purchasing a wireless 'capsule', to fit into the end of the microphone to convert it into a wireless unit.

Believe it or not, your microphone cord is an important part of stage performance. Go to YouTube and watch a few videos by Guns N' Roses. You'll notice that Axl Rose often swings his microphone by the cord. This can work into your stage moves as well. Make sure your mic is plugged in securely and that you have a good cable attached to it because if it's a cheap one, you could break the internal wiring and lose microphone signal. And in case you need to switch cables on the spot, it's not a good idea to duct tape the cord to your mic.

5. Using a microphone stand

The right microphone stand is usually a matter of taste. Make sure it's been adjusted to your correct height and tightened before you start performing or it may start sliding down in the middle of your song. As we've mentioned, some singers like to swing the microphone around by the cord when they perform. Others prefer a wireless microphone and a stand. This way they can swing just the

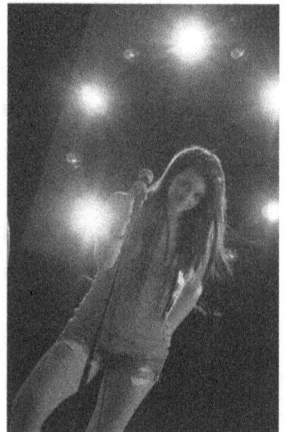

stand around in the air. Our advice is that you practice with both until you find out what works best for you.

6. Monitors

Singers definitely need to be able to hear themselves on stage. There are a variety of stage monitors that can be used to give you good feedback of your sound. Monitors are usually provided by the venue and can include big wedge monitors that sit on the stage in front of the performer, or smaller monitors mounted on stands at ear level. Monitors that fit inside the ear are also a great choice, but quite expensive.

The most cost-effective choice is called the Vocal Acoustic Monitor. The VAM is a great way to hear your own voice. It's perfect for practicing with your band and also in live situations. The worst thing you can do is sing louder when you cannot hear yourself. This will only end up making you sing out of tune, or worse, cause irritation and damage to the vocal cords. A VAM will prevent this from happening because it delivers your true vocal sound directly from your mouth to your ear.

The VAM is a MUST for all *Sing Out Loud* users because it can be used as a basic handheld practice device for doing both vocal exercises, and live performances. To purchase your VAM, go to vamcoustics.com. Don't forget to tell the owner, Byron Cancelmo, that we sent you.

7. Vocal Effects

If you want to tweak your voice to sound better, you need your own vocal effects unit. We personally suggest the vocal effects line from TC Helicon, which includes a wide variety of stage effects for singers. Most of their effects processors can run anywhere from $249.00 and up, but for an affordable price, the VoiceTone singles, which run around $149.00 per pedal are quite effective and allow you to add to your collection of effects pedals as you need and can afford. Visit them at tc-helicon.com to learn more about their products.

If you wish to experiment with effects on a lower budget and you have an iPhone or iPad, then you're in luck. TC-Helicon also makes the VoiceJam app, which is a vocal recorder/looper. The VoiceJam allows you to build a symphony of sound using your own voice. VoiceJam also features an in-app purchase for add-ons like the Hard Tune & Pitch Correction. We're sure they'll eventually carry all the VoiceTone singles through this app as well.

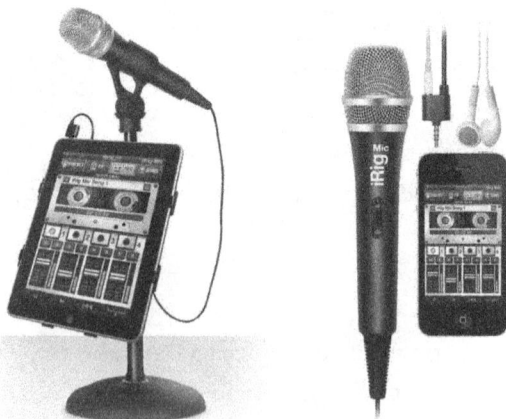

Another great app for the iPhone and the iPad is the VocaLive from IK Multimedia. VocaLive features a variety of vocal effects including seven quality studio effects and five vocal effects. You can download the free version to try out several of the effects before you decide to buy. VocaLive also features an audio recorder that can be expanded to a multi-track recorder via in-app purchase. IK Multimedia also makes the iRig mic, which is the first hand-held condenser microphone for the iPhone/iPad.

Speaking of microphones, the Mikey, by Blue Microphones is another great microphone made for the iPhone. It is a great choice if you plan to record video and wish to capture better audio sound, or it can be used with the above-mentioned apps as well.

Now let's move on to the final assignment.

Assignment #11—Working with Your Microphone

Time to incorporate your new microphone and stand technique into your daily mirror routine. Continue working on your moves in the mirror, but now you must start thinking of your microphone as an extension of your voice. Hold your microphone out (as if extending it to the crowd), twirl the stand around, hold it up high, and then lean back with the microphone in your hand. Once you feel comfortable with all these moves, we'll go to the next chapter where we'll tell you how to take it to the stage.

Chapter 3
Conquering Performance Jitters

If you've been following your assignments, then technically you've already performed in front of a crowd—

What's that you say?

You're not ready to sing in front of a live crowd yet?

Hmm, sounds like you've got a bad case of stage fright. Well, don't sweat it; almost everyone gets nervous before a performance. The trick is to transmute that panicky feeling into one of "excitement" then you can use the nervous energy to your advantage. If you recall what we said earlier, excitement and nervousness affect the body in the exact same way. It's only our perception of that burst of energy and racing heart that affects the outcome. So now we present to you the seven-step system for beating stage fright:

1. **Know your song(s)!** Uncontrolled tension both physically and mentally are the enemies of every singer. If you allow the emotional tension and nervousness to grow out of proportion, it will turn into paralyzing stage fright. You'll forget the words, your throat will dry out and you won't be able to perform well. But don't panic. There's a positive side to this story. Nervousness is energy you can use to fuel your stage performance and make you an even better artist. Nervousness happens to most performers, but the trick to overcoming it is in knowing your material. Know your songs forward and backward, up and down, inside and out; in other words, know your material REALLY, REALLY WELL. Song map and performance map all your songs. If you haven't practiced your material thoroughly, then you can easily go sharp or flat when you sing, and hearing yourself make these kinds of mistakes will only add to the nervousness you're already feeling. That's why when you feel that terrible sense of panic, being prepared will let cellular memory take over. Like being on autopilot, it will keep you on pitch and in the right tempo.

2. **Don't worry, be happy!** Stage fright is indeed a horrible sensation but the initial nervous energy you feel when you first start performing can actually supercharge your performance and turn you into a superstar performer. Before you go on stage, think about a particular time when you felt happy and excited— powerful even. That energy is similar to the sensation of stage fright. View stage fright as a happy thing. If you still need a confidence boost, try this. Before making your appearance, lightly tap your thigh, breathe in slowly and deeply and think about the rhythm of your first song. Do this repeatedly until you begin to relax and feel better. The action of having to focus on thigh-tapping and deep breathing pulls attention away from your out-of-control nervousness. Continue to breathe deeply as this is important in overcoming anxiety—it's as important as making sure you've warmed up your voice. You did warm up your voice, didn't you?

3. **If you forget your lyrics, just fake it and move on!** If in the middle of your performance you forget a word or phrase, don't become focused on thinking about the lyrics; make up words and move through the error as quickly as you can. If you dwell on it you'll forget the rest of the song. Hey, don't forget, you could even hold your microphone out to the audience and let them sing along for a few lines. The audience will love this, and that way it will cover up your mistake. The important thing is to keep your voice and your mind flowing so you can finish the song. You don't want to pull yourself out of the "moment" and start singing from your head and not your heart—the place where passion and emotion lie.

4. **Just Sing!** The main secret to a good performance is in being able to concentrate on enjoying the moment, not on HOW you are doing in that moment. In other words don't focus on your vocal technique during a live performance, just "sing". And don't get lost in your head. If you focus on the *Sing Out Loud* techniques during your daily practice, it will soon become second nature and you won't have to think about it once you start to perform; it will just happen naturally.

5. **Visualize!** Visualization is more important during live performance than focusing on the correct vocal technique. If you imagine yourself giving a great performance, then you will. In fact, right before you go on stage, see it as though it has already happened. Take a few deep breaths, a swig of water, do lip bubbles to calm down, and visualize the crowd absolutely loving you. Most performers are uptight, nervous, or full of anxiety before they hit the stage, and this includes your favorite stars. If they didn't have that nervous energy they'd be very boring on stage, so approach nervous energy as a welcomed friend.

6. **Don't listen to the negative voice!** That infernal, internal critic in your head is simply the immature part of you that wants to control the outcome. It has no business on stage with you. That brat can become extremely destructive if you allow it to take over. Some common remarks the brat will make are, "What on earth makes you think you can sing?" or "Watch out, you're not going to hit that high note" or "The crowd thinks you stink", and on and on. Send that dude (or dudette) on vacation before you make your entrance. If the brat turns up in the middle of your performance, kick it in the butt and send it packing. Hey, you can even do a real kick on stage as part of your act and no one will know you're kicking a troublemaker into the wings.

7. **The ultimate herbal stage fright remedy!** While waiting to go on stage, try a few sprays of Bach's Rescue Remedy. Rescue

Remedy is a non-toxic flower essence that will help put you into a natural state of calm. It can be purchased at most health food stores.

So follow these seven steps to eliminate stage fright and you'll conquer it in a very short time. Keep remembering that YOU are the superstar and YOU own the stage. Now that you've got those butterflies under control, you're on your way to winning millions of fans.

Chapter 4
Taking Care of Your Instrument

Although you're on your way to becoming an amazing singer, it doesn't begin and end with practice. Keep in mind that you are at all times a singer. That means when you're at school, when you're sleeping, when you're reading aloud at a poetry class, and when you're working at an after-school job, you are first and foremost, a singer. Take your voice and your body into consideration at all times so you never abuse either of them. Your voice is your instrument and you should honor it.

Another thing to remember is that the voice is an electromagnetic instrument and must be energized in order to work properly. By increasing the energy in your body, staying in shape, eating right, working out and having a cheerful attitude, you'll increase the electromagnetic energy that allows you to sing with feeling, passion and power.

The ancient Greeks believed that the greatest musical instrument of all was the voice!

The voice is the barometer of your soul so if you're feeling sad or angry or scared, these emotions will come out in your voice and mirror your state of mind. This can make your voice warble when you sing and create an unbalanced shaky sound. Try to remember that a balanced body creates a comfortable and pleasant voice to listen to, whether you're singing or speaking.

Beyond your mental attitude is basic vocal health. There'll be times when you're sick, have stuffy sinuses, a sore throat, lots of phlegm, but you still have to perform. You CAN perform when sick, unless you have laryngitis—an infection of the vocal cords. In that case, you should not sing at all.

But who wants to perform when they're sick, right? Better to stay healthy, take preventative measures and not get sick. There are many things that affect the voice and zap the energy levels needed to produce good vocal energy. The following is the basic *Sing Out Loud* list of do's and don'ts. For a more in-depth review of vocal health refer to *Raise Your Voice Second Edition*. The following points are meant as a guideline to help you keep your voice in shape not to treat or diagnose any condition you may be experiencing:

DO'S

Drink Water

And we mean tons of it. Singers need half their body weight in ounces of water every day. So if you weigh one hundred pounds, you need at least fifty ounces of water every day. Water is the creative oil a singer needs to keep the voice hydrated and the cords lubricated.

If the cords aren't lubricated, they will become dry as they vibrate together. This will result in irritation and swelling and affect your pitch and tone quality. So start drinking lots of H_2O. Whenever you practice or perform you should ALWAYS have plenty of water handy by your side.

Make sure the water is at room temperature because if it's cold, it will make the vocal cords tense up. Even better for your voice is to drink warm water, which you could keep in a thermos bottle. Sweeten it slightly with honey if you don't like the bland taste.

Other ways to keep the vocal cords and pharynx moist is by breathing steam. You can do this either by turning the shower on hot, or buying a humidifier so you can breathe steam while you sleep. Gargling water while sustaining the sound of an "aaaahhh" is good for the voice too. In fact, it's not only good for moistening the throat, but can help relieve the pain of a sore throat. This gargling action is also a great warm-up before a rehearsal or show.

Voice Sprays

Very few throat sprays are good for singers. Most contain alcohol, which dries out the throat. Anything with Eucalyptus or Menthol also dries out the throat. While there are a few decent sprays on the market for singers like **Vocal-Eze** (travelwellness.com) and **Throat Saver** (superiorvocalhealth.com), an alternative is to inhale mist by spraying water in your mouth. Fill a spray bottle with filtered water and spray it in your throat as you inhale. This will allow the water to go down and land on the vocal cords to help moisten them. You can see Abby spraying water in her throat in the picture below. It's best to use a smaller, one-ounce bottle, but the size she's using will still do the same job.

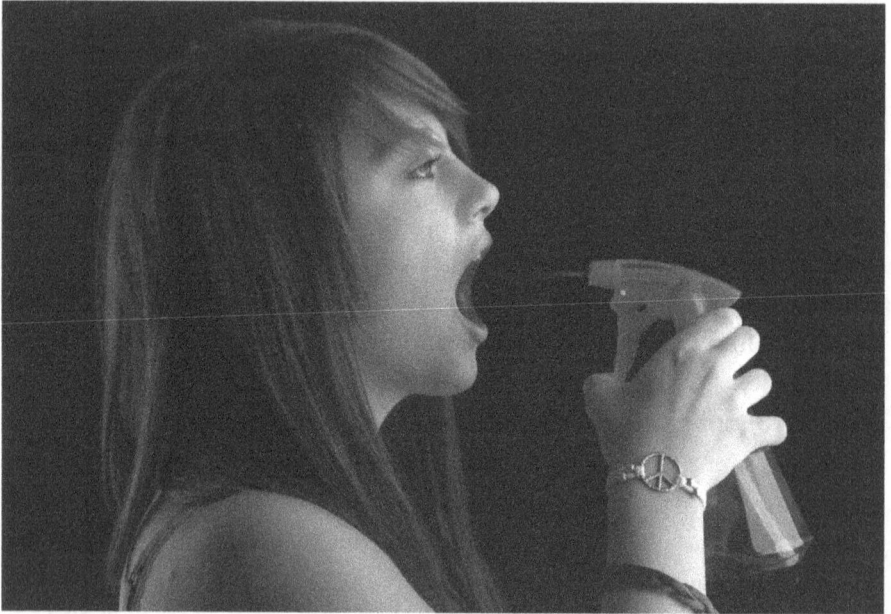

Teas
Sip herbal teas but make sure they come WITHOUT caffeine. The best teas for singers contain Slippery Elm or Licorice. Slippery Elm coats the throat and Licorice reduces swelling. One of the best teas for singers is **Throat Coat Tea** by Traditional Medicinals. You can pick up a box at most local grocery or health food stores.

Vitamins, Minerals and Herbs
While we could go into a whole list of good supplements, we're only going to cover a few here. Everyone should have a daily multiple vitamin to supply the body with much needed nutrients along with the following four other nutrients:

- **Ginseng-**If you feel like you need an energy boost and are stuck on caffeine, try Ginseng, which is a natural energy booster. Add a few drops of liquid Ginseng to juice or non-caffeinated soda as this is a much better choice to give an energy boost. You can even try a glass of apple juice, which can turbo-charge the body in the same way.

- **Vitamin C**—This vitamin is important for singers because it helps prevent colds.

- **Calcium**—Another important mineral to help prevent colds.

- **Zinc**—This is considered the singer's mineral because it helps reduce swelling around the voice. The best zinc tablets to use are the chalky kind that dissolve in your mouth, NOT Zinc Glutamate, which is like candy.

Diet

While this is not a diet book it's important to note that the old adage is true—*you are what you eat*. If you eat tons of sugar, refined white flour, or salt, you will deplete your energy, clog up your digestive system, and raise your blood pressure. This may not seem so important when you're a teenager, but it will certainly make a difference as you get older, especially if you're on an exhausting tour.

We'd hate for you to have to cancel a show because you lost your voice due to a junk-food diet so it's better to eat lots of greens and whole grains. The best book you can read for a "singer's diet" is, *Never Get Another Cold* by Thomas Appell.

Exercise

The best exercises for singers are cardio and abdominal exercises. The next time you're going to practice with your band, take fifteen minutes to go out for a jog, play tennis, jump on a trampoline, skip rope, or get into some kind of activity that gets your heart pumping. You might be tired by the time you get to your singing practice, but we guarantee you will sing better. Why? Because you've got the body warmed up and blood is flowing to all components of your singing system. If you've been running on the treadmill while singing, you can probably already attest to this.

Cardio exercises help open up the sinuses, get the lungs pumping, and generally warm up the entire body. It's also important to add some strength exercises, such as push ups, sit ups for abdominal strengthening, and squats—especially if your performance involves running around the stage.

If you want to try a program specifically developed for singers, check out *12-Minute Stage Crazy* by Ryan Murdock. *12-Minute Stage Crazy* is a video download of a cardio-yoga routine that can be performed anywhere, such as in a dressing room, on-stage during sound check, or in a hotel if your band is on the road. If you can make it through the whole twelve minutes, we guarantee you'll rock on stage! The download is available at theultimatevocalworkout.com.

Sleep

Getting sufficient sleep is extremely important to a singer. If the voice is tired from lack of rest, it will show up when you sing. No late night video games on a school or work night when you need your rest. And get anywhere from seven to nine hours of sleep consistently, night after night.

If you fall behind on sleep from staying up until three in the morning on the weekend, you cannot double up on your hours the next night. The body doesn't work that way. It may take anywhere from a few days to a week to catch up on lost sleep, so be sure to get the right amount each night.

If you're having trouble getting to sleep, darken your room and make sure you have no radio or television playing in the background. Proper rest demands you have complete audio and visual silence.

Personal Hygiene

Personal hygiene is of utmost importance. This includes regularly washing your hands to keep from collecting germs, and daily baths or showers. Brush and floss your teeth and use mouthwash frequently. You don't want to develop germs in your mouth that lead to bad breath or a cold. You might also want to use a tongue scraper after brushing your teeth. This removes bacteria from the tongue and prevents germs from spreading. It will also help eliminate bad breath. Trust us; your fans won't appreciate a stinky mouth.

If you have a tendency to get a lot of sinus colds or your nose is constantly stopped up, you need to start sinus flushing, which is a technique that is thousands of years old. It's a simple way to rinse salt water through the nostrils in order to remove any debris that may cause infection. Whenever you breathe through your nose, you're collecting nearby dust and contaminates. Left in the sinuses it will irritate the nostrils, which can lead to an infection.

Sinus flushing is just as important as brushing your teeth. To flush your sinuses you'll use what is called a Neti-Pot. The best Neti-Pot to use is the Nasa Flo made by NeilMed.com. Check out their free sinus flushing "how-to" video at neilmed.com/usa/netipot_video.php. Neildmed's, Nasa mist is another way to keep the sinuses moist and clean as well.

Speaking Voice Technique

A healthy speaking voice leads to a healthy singing voice. When speaking throughout the day, you must apply the same techniques you use for singing. You must breathe correctly, add the downward support, and feel the buzz. If you speak all day long on the same pitch, the voice will become even more tired than singing.

Pretend you're a walking vocal exercise. In other words, vary your pitch as you speak. Speak some notes in a high pitch, some in a medium pitch, and some in a low pitch. Use passion in your voice when you speak, and if you put a bit of laughter into it, your words will float out of you.

If you don't feel any buzz, bend over at your hips with legs slightly bent like the opposite picture, and hum "mmmm" so you can feel it in your cheeks, nose and the roof of your mouth. Then stand up and begin speaking. You should feel the buzz now. Master your speaking voice along with your singing voice because in reality, they are one and the same.

31

Vocal Rest

If you have strained your voice, you need to take a day of vocal rest. Don't talk for an entire day and definitely stay off your cell phone. This doesn't mean you can whisper because whispering actually aggravates the vocal cords even more. It simply means taking a break from talking and maintaining absolute vocal silence to give your voice a chance to heal. If you need to say something, write it down on paper or text it.

DON'TS

Don't Smoke

Singers should never smoke. NO, NO, NO! Not ever! PERIOD. Smoking of any kind dries out the throat. Contrary to belief, smoking is NOT cool. Dry throat leads to vocal disaster. Nicotine destroys vitamin C, which we need to stay healthy. Other types of substance smoking are illegal and will over time destroy the brain. More and more cancer of the throat is being traced back to marijuana use.

Over the counter drugs

OTC drugs such as cold medicines can also dry out your throat. Yes, there are times you might need them, but try a natural herbal solution instead, and try to stay healthy by taking nutrients. This way you won't have to use OTC drugs. Remember, additives like menthol and eucalyptus can irritate a singer's throat. As mentioned before, if you have a tendency to suffer from sinus infections, flush them out rather than using a sinus inhaler. Don't use OTC sleep aids because you'll wake up with a very dry mouth. All these type of drugs are addictive and will only make matters worse. Drink more water instead.

Alcohol

We need hardly tell you how much alcohol can dry out your throat. If you drink liquor before you sing you'll most likely end up getting tipsy and slurring your words. You may even fall off the stage. This is not a cool way to gain fans.

Dairy

Dairy products like milk and cheese affect some people. If you drink milk and get lots of phlegm buildup in your throat afterwards, then avoid dairy products, especially on the day of the show.

Caffeine

Caffeine is what is known as a diuretic. It will make you pee a lot which means it will dry out your body, including your voice. Some people are more sensitive to caffeine than others. If you find yourself clearing your throat a lot after drinking coffee, tea or soda, then steer clear of these drinks. If you like the taste of something sweet or need a little energy boost, drink fruit juices with no added sugar. It will give you an energy boost from its natural sugar. You can always add a little shot of liquid ginseng to pep you up.

CONGRATULATIONS!!!

You are now on your way to becoming a super star. Keep using the *Sing Out Loud* system as your guidebook to singing and keep practicing your vocal exercises. Follow the Do's and Don'ts and before long, you'll be on stage rocking with the best of them.

Keep us informed of your progress. Email us through our websites and let us know all about your progress. We want copies of your first record, and we won't mind it in the least if you thank us in the liner notes!

Bonus: We've created a special section for our *Sing Out Loud* graduates at http://venderapublishing.com/sing-out-loud-book-four, which will be periodically updated with tips and bonuses. Check it out today!

**Well, that wraps it up for *SING OUT LOUD*.
Can't wait to see you all on stage.
Rock on!**

About the Author
Jaime Vendera

Jaime Vendera is the author of a variety of books and one of the most sought-after vocal coaches on the planet. Using the methods he created, Jaime turned his two-octave range into six octaves with massive decibels of raw vocal power that enabled him to set a world record shattering glass with his voice. When singers need more vocal range, power and projection, or need to build up vocal stamina to perform every night, they call Jaime Vendera. Jaime states that, "none of this would have been possible without God."

Ben Thomas of Dweezil Zappa says that Jaime is the 'Mr. Miyagi' of vocal coaches, while Mat Devine of Kill Hannah considers him more of a 'Yoda.' James LaBrie of Dream Theater said, "Because of my lessons with Jaime, my voice is feeling and sounding better than it has in twenty years. I am spot-on every night. He is the Vocal Guru." Myles Kennedy of Alter Bridge said, "One time during a tour, I was so sick I could barely make it through the set. It looked as if we were going to have to cancel the next show. Jaime spent some time giving me some tips that helped me regain my voice. By the next night, I was able to perform the show. He is fantastic! *Raise Your Voice Second Edition* is THE book for singers. I recommend his books and his private instruction to ALL singers." Jaime can be contacted at www.jaimevendera.com.

About the Author
Anne Loader McGee

Anne has studied with a number of well-known Hollywood singing teachers. She has performed in musical theatre productions and taken classes in songwriting, music, and film at both the American Film Institute and the University of California and Los Angeles (UCLA).

She also co-wrote *Strengthening Your Singing Voice* with Elizabeth Sabine, a voice-strengthening expert whom many famous singers, actors, and speakers have consulted over the last twenty-five years. (www.elizabethsabine.net)

As an award winning children's writer, Anne has produced plays for young people, developed animation scripts, and had a number of short stories published in magazines, and in the Los Angeles Times. Anne's middle grade novels, *The Mystery at Marlatt Manor* and *Anni's Attic* are available at Amazon and Barnes & Noble. You can find her at www.annemcgee.com.